Endorsements from "F

Ron Henderson's (Fitness King)
beyond the gym. I have trained ~~g~~ ... ~~years and plan~~
to stay young with his help for many years to come. I have spent twenty years
building a business and putting other parts of my life on hold. Ron has helped me
get into better physical condition than when I was twenty years old. My training
with Ron has helped me make better decisions in reference to nutrition and also
in reference to my cardio training. The King's influence helped me make the
decision to no longer consume alcohol. The impact on my life has been very
positive. I talk to my employees on how life-changing this experience has been.
I hope to expose as many friends and coworkers as possible to his approach to
living.

Wade Davis, Executive Vice President
Financial Recovery Services, Inc.

At the first meeting he's the drill instructor out of Central Casting, but don't let
appearances fool you. This man houses the simplest/complex personality you
can conjure. Ron, the "Fitness King" to most, has an enthusiasm which brings
physical and mental strength to his clients. *"Keep those legs strong,"* he says,
"they are going to have to carry you the rest of your life." His credos are brief:
"Eat sensibly, sleep well, and get your aerobics in; a simple format for sure.
What works for him will work for you; he is never sick, never late and never
self indulges. Ron Henderson is a man of his word, a man of faith and one who
has given to many by his example through his lifestyle. I am approaching my
seventieth birthday and will have been with Ron twelve years and offer the above
feelings with much experience and am proud to call him, "friend."

John Rimarcik, Minneapolis Restaurant Operator

Endorsements Continued

My experience with the Fitness King has left me with many lessons that I will carry with me for years to come. When I first started to train with him, he asked me, "What is it that you are trying to do; what kind of physique are you looking for?" I told him, and that's exactly what he delivered… and a little bit more. I'm always traveling, so I told the Fitness King that I won't always have the best equipment to choose from for my workouts, and in that case, I want some very basic exercises, as well, so there will be no excuse for me not to workout. Two chairs, the floor, a desk, a giant rubber band–to name a few–are simple everyday things that made very big changes in my life. I learned to become more focused, concentrated and more intense with each muscle group. So my results came quickly. I have always been told by my parents, "Health is wealth." I finally know what that means. The Fitness King believes this as well.

Stokley, with "Mint Condition"
of the International Recording Group

What is obvious is that trainers train what they have learned. I was using trainers that thought that building bulk and being able to lift more and more is a good thing. I had to buy bigger shirts as I became bigger and heavier. I had to buy bigger weights. When I made a change I was using 70 and 75 pound dumbbells. It was impressive to everyone watching as these huge weights went up and down. My weight was up but so was my blood pressure. Ron changed my point of view. Reps count and weight is not so important. After three years, I am down 25 pounds and feel lean and trim. I have done this without an injury. So why do I go through all of this? The real answer is obvious: to live longer and maintain the quality of my life now and in the future. I've worked hard my whole life to enjoy the years that I've accumulated some money. Without a body that could do the things I enjoy, the money would not be very useful or fun.

Mark Saliterman, Certified Public Accountant
Saliterman, Ries, & Almquist, LTD.

"What is it worth for you to become

Physically Fit?"

RON HENDERSON
The Fitness King
Author, Motivator, Personal Fitness Trainer

What is it worth for you to become

Physically Fit?

RON HENDERSON
The Fitness King
Author, Motivator, Personal Fitness Trainer

A Life-Changing Book from River City Press, Inc.

ISBN No. 0-9776713-6-4

COVER PHOTO
Rick Busch
Minneapolis, MN

PHOTO CONCEPT
Grossman Design
St. Louis Park, MN.

GRAPHIC LAYOUT
Sara Jo Johnson
Roseville, MN

EDITOR
Amy Roster
Duluth, MN

PUBLISHER
River City Press, Inc.
4301 Emerson Avenue North
Minneapolis, MN 55412
1-888-234-3559
publisher@rivercitypress.net
www.rivercitypress.net

Acknowledgements

I want to thank my Lord and Savior for inspiring and guiding me to write this book. Without Him, this book could not be written. Also for the gift God placed within me to encourage, train and help people to reach and exceed their fitness goals.

My love and thanks to my wife Dinah for understanding my early morning wake-ups and late, late nights given to my writing. Also, to my first child, Mason Lee. He was a catalyst for me to start writing and also to write a children's book, now in the works. Thanks to Majestic Lee and Brandon Liam for their energy and zest for the physical things in life.

Thanks also to all my clients who, through the years, have allowed me the privilege to train them. With them I continue to learn and perfect the methods needed for them to realize their desired fitness goals.

My parents, Russell and Rachel, inspired me by example. They believed enough in fitness to actually practice it in their lives, influencing me to develop a passion to stay fit and become a trainer.

Thanks to my friend Curt Lund from Spiritual Life Church for introducing me to Bob Wolf, CEO of River City Press, Inc. who sees the need in our society for a book like "What is it worth for you to become Physically Fit?"

A special thanks to my good friends, Steve Shapiro from French Meadows Bakery and Otis Courtney of Courtney International; both of these men have believed in me and have supported me in many thoughtful ways. Also to the men's group and the Pastors at Spiritual Life Church in Brooklyn Park, Minnesota for their spiritual guidance and   prayer support.

My two previous pastors (before joining my current church) also were very helpful to my spiritual growth. Thanks to Pastor Randy Morrison. Randy is Senior Pastor at "Speak The Word Church

International" in Golden Valley, MN. My other previous Pastor is Jay Neu, Senior Pastor of Living Water Christian Church of Hopkins, MN. Blessings to you, Pastor Jay.

A very special thanks to the many clients who have taken time to contribute to this venture with personal testimonies and endorsements, telling of their experiences for you to review through this book. A special acknowledgement to my many friends who allowed me to read to them parts of this manuscript as it was being crafted. Blessings to each and everyone of you!

Forward

Mark Rosen

Take it from one who knows…

One of my favorite sayings I often repeat comes from my friend and Channel 4 anchor, Don Shelby, who said, "We are fugitives from the law of averages."

Yes, as I sit here in my fifty-fourth year on Earth, I often think how many times I've been in the right place at the right time, surviving close calls that I'm probably not even aware of.

Ron Henderson has helped me increase those odds with his insatiable passion for improving my personal health. We are all so busy in our 24-7 world of cell phones, instant messaging and lap top computers. Heck, we can order a cup of coffee through a drive thru window. Are we really that busy?

Too busy to take care of our personal health with simple every day commitments?

There are dozens of fitness books and DVDs available at your fingertips, but there is only one "Fitness King," Ron Henderson, who can show you easy steps to improving your physical and mental health.

I've been blessed with thirty plus years doing exactly what I've wanted to do as a sports broadcaster.

Ron Henderson has taught me the right preparation to enjoy the next thirty years of my life with my health as the number one priority. Now that's advice you can take to the bank. I like my odds!

Mark Rosen
WCCO TV Sports Director

The Author's Passion

The inspiration to write this book, came from a deep longing and calling in my heart to help people realize their physical potential. I've observed that the average man or woman fifty years or older coming to my office has never had a consistent exercise program. As a result, most people come in poor physical condition. Truly, I hope my story will inspire many to find real joy in just being alive! I struggled intensely to get and stay in shape as a young man. My main reason, though I had many good ones, was that I was so sick and tired of not feeling good physically and mentally.

During my high school years, I was on the wrestling team and learned how good it felt to be alert and active when physically in shape. The intense training they put you through quickly gets you through the doldrums and soon feeling better rather than just dragging yourself through the day.

Unfortunately, as soon as wrestling season ended, I quickly went back to my old ways of not working out and eating too much of the wrong foods. This went on a few times-in and out of shape-my belly getting bigger, gaining extra weight and losing my stamina. One day I woke up and decided "enough is enough." I made a commitment that as long as I lived, to get in shape and not allow myself to lose it all again if I could help it. Here it is thirty-three years later and I've kept my promise to myself. Today, I have never felt physically better. In fact, there are physical activities that I could not do when I was twenty-six that I can do now.

All this is said to let you know it is worth working for and your long term health dividends that you need and want are within your reach. Now at age fifty-two my waist size and weight are the same as they were in 1976. My personal physical investment returned dividends–more than I can count. I'm healthy and feel like a million dollars…you can too.

For almost three decades I have served as a personal fitness trainer for the young and old. Many clients served are medical professionals, athletes, executives, retired seniors, mechanics, people in the trades and business owners. They are people who decided they want to stay physically active as long as possible. How about you?

Contents

If you are determined to succeed to become and stay physically fit, you must realize it will take a very serious desire and whole hearted commitment to keep at it as a choice for a lifetime. If you are married, I suggest you discuss it fully with your spouse. This is something you should consider doing together. Make a joint commitment for each of you to get fit and stay fit all your lives together.

Your determination and enthusiasm may convince your partner to get fit with you. Together your commitment will strengthen and insure both of you to have a better chance to reach your goals. Work at it until it becomes a habit. Should your partner slack off, don't give up. You owe it to yourself to stay the course. Your consistency to keep at it will help your spouse to stay involved.

Remember how tough it was to start saving money? It is important to get into the habit of depositing a little on a regular basis. It pays off as your total grows and the interest earnings increase. Start together. Put regular deposits into your fitness account and the dividends earned will help insure your willingness to keep on with your fitness program. When it comes to your health, what is the right amount to deposit? Doesn't that depend where you are physically with your health? One thing for sure, if you are ready to start an exercise program, plan on checking with your doctor. If he gives you the "go-ahead," let your body and common sense become your guide.

I remember riding my bike over twenty-three years ago when I had an accident. Someone opened a car door and I hit it. I flew off my bike and hit the ground very hard; my pain was so intense from the fall that I didn't work out for almost a whole year. When I finally did start again, it was like starting over from the beginning. I would pick a couple of body parts to work on and then only do about two or three sets for each muscle group.

Before being injured, I was working twelve to fifteen repetitions for each set. After three or four weeks of low intensity workouts, I could add a few more repetitions to my workout account to get back to my potential. It's just like what I do with my IRA; I keep putting in reasonable amounts for both my financial and health accounts for use in later years.

Planning to live a long, healthy, and prosperous life is not enough…you have to do something about it.

We started this first chapter with the focus on our attitudes and choices. Please consider the following:

Your dividends earned in your health account become <u>some of your most valuable possessions</u>!

What is the largest amount of money you earned from an investment? Think about it…..

Now visualize yourself, age fifty, laying in a hospital room, with the best doctors around you that money can buy. They don't know what to do next, and you hear them whisper, "I don't know why people do not take care of themselves – they don't need to end up here."

How much money would you invest in your health now to get back what you lost by lack of balanced priorities?

It becomes a simple answer: "Everything we have."

Seek to develop a moderate and balanced life style.

We have been conditioned to get out of balance with the over emphasis of our careers and the drive to make money as the most important thing in our lives. Think about it.

From what you have read so far, I now want you to consider how important your attitude and choices affect you, your children, and spouse.

Make a commitment to yourself, as I did years ago, to become fit and stay healthy as long as it is possible. It's a wise choice that none of us will ever regret.

Many of us are drowning financially; we are way over our heads in bills and debt. It is at times like this that a good financial planner can be a life saver. Once we realize this, the quicker we can solve the problem, the better. In our present culture, the normal demands of life put most of us in a stressed out position even when we are financially solvent.

Many of us are drowning physically because of our poor eating habits, over indulgence of beer, wine, alcohol, and a stressed out, overworked life. We need to be educated, motivated and committed to change. It's in times like this that a doctor, personal trainer, and a nutritionist can be a lifesaver.

Living the high life may look good on the outside but eventually it will catch up to all of us. Too many of us are physically destroying our bodies, taking years off our life span because of excessive, undisciplined lifestyles with no physical activities.

It's well proven, that exercise, a moderate lifestyle and a healthy diet are like a lifeline to a drowning person. We have to grab the line to keep from drowning from our excessive, out of balance bad habits and careless living.

When we are burdened down with bills, it will affect our living status…When we are excessively over weight, it affects our whole life status and can be the beginning of serious health problems. Being seriously overweight can shorten your life span. No matter how smart you are, a great mind cannot operate out of a dead body.

Broke But Not Physically Broken…

There are times when you have no available cash. When you have no immediate means to get cash, you could say that you are cash poor, financially speaking.

If you have made investments, such as property, stocks and bonds, jewelry, classic cars, you are obviously not bankrupt. When you are walking around out of shape, overweight and thinking just because you can still move, you are just fine–don't fool yourself. Anyone in this condition is broke, physically speaking. Not bankrupt yet, but physically broke.

You can fix the problem by making good deposits into your health savings accounts by eating sensibly and exercising your body. Start watching what and how much you eat and how you invest your time. This is how to start remedying the problem of being physically poor.

You've heard the term cash poor; well, I've been cash poor a few times in my life, but I have kept myself from becoming physically poor for over thirty-four years. Let's face it, if we are not watching what we spend our cash on most of the time, then we are watching what our wives or husbands are spending. Unless, of course, there is so much cash it makes no difference what you buy. If we could be half as aware of our physical health as our finances, we would be on our way to becoming physically fit and health conscious. Take the first step in the direction of moderation and practice it in all that you do.

Moderation is a common word with great significance. Imagine where we'd all be if we practiced moderation in all that we think and do. We would not be overweight, as we would not be overeating, nor selecting the too-fatty foods. We would not have two sets of clothes in our closets–one for the bigger and smaller me. We would have more energy and be able to move more and be less tired.

I look at moderation as being balanced. When we monitor our check books and keep them balanced, life is good and our creditors are happy. When we make sure we do our yearly exams with our doctors, our family is happy and we are in a better position to ward off any possible health maladies.

A case study in moderation and commitment

For a period of two years, I had a woman come and train with me who was physically broke! She was close to bankruptcy. At roughly 5 feet 6 inches tall, she weighed over 320 pounds. She could barely bend over to tie her shoes. She could barely breathe with any physical activity.

After her first year training with me, she lost 100 pounds. She worked on weights three times a week and she walked on the treadmill two to three days on her own as well. She developed vigor and energy and now smiles because of reaching a physically solvent point in her life.

She is at an all time high with her physical net worth being up there with the best. This smart lady practices moderation in all parts of her life and has won the battle for physical independence. How did she do so well?

Simple. It all started when she decided to train with me as her body banker (personal trainer) and took small but significant steps towards investing in her health and well being.

These have power over us when we allow them

Food is what we <u>make it</u>	Money is anything <u>we allow it to be</u>
For most a necessity	For most a necessity
Some a way of life	Some it's their life
To some an award	For some it's power
Many are addicted	Many are addicted
Others find escape	Others find freedom

What do you allow these to be?
Can you change and
take charge of your life?

See what a couple of people whom I've trained have to say…

The "Fitness King" changed my life forever by redefining the quality of life. Before I met Ron Henderson, my lifestyle was centered on Profit and

Loss. I started a company from scratch in 2,000 and dedicated all my time and attention to "growing the business." As such, words like, "Passion, Tenacity, Sacrifice, Drive, Health, Repetition, Performance, Execution, Benefits, Stamina and Balanced Results," were all words that described my dedication to the success and expansion of my healthy business today.

These were, however, not the words I used to define the health of my body.

Now having worked for over a year with the "King," I feel energized, rejuvenated and younger than I ever have before. And most of all, I understand the merits of maintaining a balanced life.

I live a more fit, productive, and fulfilled life today because of this shift in my priorities. Achieving a more balanced life resulted in a greater 'quality of life.' This is a goal many strive to accomplish, but few actually realize in their lifetime. For this I have the Fitness King to thank. Your unbridled dedication to my life goals has not gone unnoticed. I look forward to the next 25 years of work and fitness.

Thanks, "King,"
Steve Wagenheim, President
Granite City Food & Brewery

Chapter Two

Benefits

You never knew were possible...

God gave us each a body which is a biological masterpiece in which our soul and spirit reside. The choice is ours to keep body, mind and spirit fit and take care of it or to abuse it by our habits and the lives we choose to live. No matter what the age or condition your body is in right now, there is hope and help for great improvement. Our bodies make miraculous progress towards fitness when consistent care is received. Think about the following reasons you may want to consider getting and staying healthy with a personal trainer.

Ten reasons why you may need a Fitness Planner/ Trainer

1. You think you are too old to work out.

2. You are in poor physical condition.

3. You've trained for years but have reached a plateau.

4. You're injury prone.

5. You're not excited about it; you need motivation.

6. You have done it for a while but with no results.

7. The discipline of one-on-one makes you accountable.

8. A fitness planner can help you maximize each workout.

9. A fitness trainer will know what exercises work best for you.

10. Your cat can beat you at arm wrestling.

To obtain desired results, plan on a minimum of three workout sessions each week. You will need consistency to have lifetime habits developed for your ongoing fitness.

My suggestion to the person seeking to develop personal fitness is to connect with a professional personal trainer. If you think this is a self-serving suggestion, my response is, "Of course it is." I know that I will make a positive difference in seeing my clients develop an effective and highly-focused training plan that will last for the rest of their life. It's a fact, or I would not have earned the reputation with my clients that I now enjoy.

Like any other important investment, it is wise to approach with caution. Compare your options. I have learned, what is important for optimal results, from working with hundreds of clients in nearly three decades of one-on-one personal training encounters. Let me share some thoughts with you that will make a world of difference for a successful relationship with your selection of a personal trainer.

Qualities of a good Professional Fitness Trainer:

- The trainer has good listening and communication skills.

- The trainer is honest and truthful.

- The trainer is cautious and recommends only what is best for the client.

- The trainer encourages feed back and assesses progress as the client develops.

- The trainer has a perfectionistic attitude while instructing his clients.

- The trainer is detailed and organized to assist clients in reaching their peak.

- The trainer keeps him or herself in great condition.

- The trainer cares more about YOU than making money.

How to find a good Fitness Trainer

If you belong to a health club, you may find a good trainer who is dedicated to his or her clients. Unfortunately, you may find that not all trainers are highly motivated though, as a regular club employee. Within a club, the wage or salary is usually not based on how well a client is doing.

I have found that more of the better trainers seek to work on their own-independently from any club. Motivation seems to be at much higher levels with self-employed individuals. When you work on your own, the only way to keep your client coming back is to keep producing positive results. Make sense?

In the quest to find the fitness trainer best for you, I suggest asking a variety of people about who they would recommend. A good fitness trainer will have a reputation and a relationship with his or her clients because of the professional ability, personal interest and concern extended.

It's important to be cautious when selecting a trainer. Whether you are considering a trainer with a health club or one that is self-employed, be careful. A younger trainer may not have the experience that a seasoned trainer will have. From my personal experience, I know it takes many years to get to the point when, instinctively, you really know how and what needs to be done, while you are still learning.

How to connect with a Professional Trainer

First, on the agenda, is for you to check in with your personal physician and have an exam to be advised what you should or should not do to begin an exercise program. It is always important to start slowly with any program to avoid hurting yourself.

When you meet with a trainer you will answer a variety of questions about prior injuries or physical limitations. It takes a variety of questions and tests to check your cardio conditioning, strength, flexibility and how many times you've started exercise programs and prematurely quit. A good trainer wants to know your personal habits concerning eating, smoking and drinking. Also important are your personal fitness goals as to desired weight, appearance, strength and stamina. This is necessary to determine if anything could curtail or hinder you from meeting your fitness goals.

Once the information is obtained, a trainer can design a program that will meet your desired physical needs, lifestyle, time schedule and level of commitment. If you do decide to use a trainer, he or she would start you out slowly until you develop the habit of exercising. When a habit is formed, it will become a lifestyle with long term benefits.

You will find many correlations with the development of your health and fitness account to investing money in a bank savings account and stock savings plans. You have to start where you are currently and move forward. Buying this book is a good step forward in the right direction. I hope it is a catalyst to get you and those close to you on the road toward physical independence.

Benefits I've observed watching clients develop physically

Slowing down the aging process...

A friend and client of mine whom I will call Dr. John for privacy's sake, is one of the top doctors in his field of expertise in Minnesota. Dr. John has been training with me for over twenty-one years. One of the most impressive things is, *he looks younger now than when he first started.* In fact, I have a photo of him that I took when he started training with me. When people see this early picture they almost always say he looks like sixty to sixty-five years old back then. Amazingly today this man is in his sixties now but looks younger than the day he started to workout. I say this to let you know you do not have to look your age to be in poor health. When you become physically fit, truly you can slow down the aging process–if not reverse it–if you take time to consistently exercise while you are young.

Greater resistance to health issues...

I have a friend who is the number one sports anchor in Minnesota with WCCO–Mark Rosen. Mark trained with me well over twelve years. When we first met, it seemed like every third or fourth week he was getting sick, or catching a cold. When he was sick, it usually took him a long time to get over it. Since Mark's fitness has improved, if he becomes sick, it doesn't last as long as before. He has developed a greater energy level and feels better most of the time. This man, like many others, has proven that regular exercise not only makes you look and feel better, but boosts your immune system also.

Untapped power keeps on flowing…

One of my original mentors to motivate me was Jack LaLanne, a real fitness role model. For as long as I can remember as a young child, I would wake up early in the morning to see Jack LaLanne. I have never met Jack personally. For years I watched him do push-ups, pull ups, or jumping jacks which became his trademark. He could do almost anything. While watching TV, I would try to follow his moves–each with boundless energy. He just kept on going, on and on. For years, I watched and learned early how to do basic exercises and found it fun and interesting.

What I liked most about Jack, was that he lived what he preached. I, too, seek to live what I preach, and I wouldn't write a fitness book without mentioning Jack LaLanne because he set many great examples of what it means to be physically independent. Jack has stayed on a life-long plan to stay physically free and today, in his nineties, he looks twenty years younger and still exercises with a healthy, fit body. Also Jack is very financially fit.

See, you can have both wealth and health. If you could only have one, which would you choose? Hopefully, the latter.

The lady from Sweden leaves a healthy legacy…

On a cold November morning sitting in a local coffee shop writing, I noticed a fit and healthy looking woman getting a cup of coffee. As she passed my table, I stopped her to ask what she did to stay in shape. I was very surprised when she replied she runs, and lifts weights. I told her I was very impressed and asked her how long she had been consistently exercising.

Her reply was since she was twenty-eight years old. She said she had been doing this for twenty years as she now was forty-eight. She looked much younger. I asked if her parents were also physically fit, and she said, "No they are not; my dad did financially well but his health is a mess." She continued, "That's why my daughter and granddaughter exercise." They have picked up on her good habits and they also are into running. Before she left, I asked how working out made her feel? She replied, "I am very happy to have an influence on my daughter and others around me. I have much more peace and am mentally and socially active as well."

No need to reinvent the wheel to become physically fit

Almost all financially well-off families have done some or all of the following to gain their present position in life.

1. Paid themselves first

Many invest in property or land and learned to let their money work for them instead of working for their money.

2. They took time now to invest in their health

If you invest time, energy and yes, some money now into your health while you still have it, in time your health will work for you by providing you with a fit body which is more self sufficient and less reliant on health care aid providers. Today is a good day to start thinking seriously about starting some type of body investment program while you physically can. When you get older, you won't lament over the fact you didn't make the effort to invest in yourself. Most of us make excuse after excuse for not getting important things done. This is one area excuses won't hold water. We need to pay ourselves first in our physically fit account if we expect to be there physically and mentally for our children and spouses through the tough times.

3. They made automatic direct deposits

In the financial world, when you're not in the habit of saving money, one of the easiest ways to save is through automatic deductions. You decide up front to have money put aside from your check for an easier way to save. It is a clear cut way to save and increase your cash for a specific purpose. This relates to the physical world as well to get started on your physical well-being.

4. They made commitments to their health

Get all the preliminary details in place, connect with a good trainer, choose to make the commitment to get on your way with consistent workout sessions and keep your appointments. Mark off the times in advance in your appointment book and work the rest of your life experiences around this vital commitment for your good health. Make it a habit. Good health is like a credit card account…you are either behind or up to date. Keep your health account paid up in full!

Be open to the investment opportunity of a lifetime…
Wanted–Serious Investors Only

How would you respond when a trusted friend calls you and says they have a great investment opportunity? One they have tried themselves and loved the payoff it earned.

It has a limited availability for investment and needs immediate attention. Would it pique your interest? The only qualifications needed to get involved and succeed in this investment is that you must be serious about it.

No cash is needed to start.

And there are no hidden charges on the investment

It is available immediately with no surprises

Tax free, low output, high yield, and no overhead

In my years, I had many investment opportunities–each and every one of them promising to be the best. Some of them seemed very good and looked like a sure thing. I did not invest in any of them. I have never regretted taking the first step towards investing in my health, and you won't either.

Cash is king…or is it?

What's $500,000 minus $300,000?
The Answer is: $200,000.

Now what's $500,000 minus your health?
The Answer: $500,000 minus your health is:

0, Nada, Nothing!

Yes, you could pile up a stack of money as high as the Statue of Liberty and you still wouldn't be close to a cure for hardening of the arteries. We know in most cases money can't buy a cure. Only the choices we make can buy us good health.   Some say that everyday above ground is a good day; I say everyday that we **increase our health dividends is a great day.**

Chapter Three

Obstacles

Learn to overcome harmful habits

An obstacle is anything that holds you back from keeping your promises or reaching your goals. We all face them in our daily challenges progressing through life. Once we have a vision and our commitment to develop a new lifestyle for improving our overall physical fitness, is solid, let's get on with it. Let's tackle the obstacles with our winning "can do" attitude.

Change the menu and lower the quantity of food intake per meal.

One of the first obstacles to being fit is being overweight. Exercise will help reduce the waistline, but it will take a life changing new habit to keep it trim. Most people find that their diet and food choices have been working against them. The first place to start is making better selections of low calorie foods and then eating smaller portions. It's okay to leave something on your plate. You can do leftovers later. Once the weight comes off, increase your muscle tone through working out. You can reshape your body and increase your energy.

Most of us are aware of the foods needed to keep us well and healthy. Also it is common knowledge that many foods now have low nutrient content. It's important to supplement our foods with quality vitamins and minerals. We'll talk more about this later.

To stay healthy we need to eat healthy! A good mixture of fruit and vegetables with fresh grown ingredients whenever possible, outperforms the packaged and fatty foods and keep us healthier as well as more active.

Excessive weight and excessive spending must be controlled.

Where is the money coming from to add on a personal trainer and whatever other expense this fitness lifestyle will cost? It's a good question that needs a real answer. Just as extra weight on our body causes extra strain, excessive spending causes strain on the whole family.

Let's start on the spending excessively first. Statistics show that the more people make, the more they desire to spend. Nowadays, most families have both spouses in the workforce.

Each has separate needs to be met to be equipped for working out of the home. There are extra costs for clothes, transportation, child care and a dozen other unplanned expenses. When the outflow of cash exceeds the inflow, important things like house payments, gas bills, lights, water bills and credit cards become a problem to keep up.

Controlling your spending is all important to keep the family in harmony. Spouses get out of sorts with each other in a hurry when the spending gets out of control. It's all about how much, over budget, is going out! If, jointly, the spending is not controlled, over time it will worsen and end in a split and bankruptcy. This course of action breaks relationships and destroys your credit ratings.

The easiest way not to get there is not to go there in the first place.

As a family, you have to develop a realistic budget and stay within its limits. Monitor your buying and spend only what you can really afford. Never write a check that you cannot cover.

This book is not about thinking properly about your finances, or budgeting your income. ***Then why all the conversation on finances? A great question.***

We are addressing this because many think everything is impossible when money is tight.

I want you to know that the answers to your problems, for the most part, are right before your eyes. You can start healing your financial problems, and every other situation when you look at it for what it is and stop doing what got you there. Take what you know about finances, saving, budgeting and investing, and apply to your whole family's health. You can be on your way to an energizing lifestyle that helps keep everyone fit and productive for a lifetime.

Usually when parents are overweight, children will become so with them. An excessively overweight person, will not have the energy needed and will be unhappy with themselves, whether it is admitted or not. This puts an undue strain on relationships. The only way for relief is to change the bad habit of excessively overeating more food than can be burned off. This habit yields a negative health flow resulting in serious, costly health problems such as coronary problems and diabetes.

Be diligent to invest in your health and the health of your family. We improve both our mental and physical health as we do this. See how important it is to develop a family fitness budget? What you pay now, you will save later.

Parents set the example to lead their children into a healthy lifestyle.

Children that see parents eating correctly and exercising consistently will follow their example. If dad complains about some of the vegetables, do you think it has an effect on the kids? Of course it does. If a parent is negative on a certain food or workout routine, the children will not want any part of it.

Current studies show that one of every three children in the U. S.–about 25 million of them–are overweight. A recent survey includes children two years of age through nineteen years old. Also, more men are obese than ever before. Obesity is a serious national health problem, Steps need to be taken to curb this trend–especially in children and teenagers.

The upward trend towards obesity in children and adults has public health officials deeply concerned and fearing an explosion of obesity-related health problems. These concerns include heart disease, cancer and Type 2 diabetes–which is already at an all time high in children.

Women are still the primary grocery shoppers and menu planners for food at home. It's important that mothers take obesity seriously and develop better selections of healthy foods that provide nutrition and build healthy bodies–with less fat content and calories.

Mom, plan a strategy to make more good foods available for our kids with hidden fruits and vegetables. Favorites that don't seem like the real thing are salsa, spaghetti sauce, vegetables in stir fry, fruit popovers, muffins, and bean burritos. Also, a variety of various vegetable soups works well. Part of a good strategy is to provide two, three or even four kinds of veggies or fruit at a time. Let the reluctant child have a couple of options.

It's important to your health also, ladies, to be serious about carrying too much weight. Proper nutrition is all important through small portions of high energy foods with low fat content. As women grow older, they need professional medical monitoring of hormones and vitamin supplements to prevent bone and muscle loss. Also, weight and strength training are important to prevent muscle and bone loss. It is very important to your daily living.

Women and men alike in their late thirties and forties begin to lose muscle. Over a ten year period a total of 2.5 pounds of muscle can be lost. This loss is a major factor in osteoporosis and bone loss.

It is proven that both men and women can shape a more attractive body through weight training and develop increased muscle where needed to support a health body with strength and vigor for an active physical life.

Meet every obstacle with a "can do" resolve.

The Marines have a policy in combat, **no man left behind.** If I had my way, I would start a national program that would help assure that no child is left *weigh* behind. What I mean by this is that no child should have to deal with being obese. Most obese children don't have to be. With a no one left behind program, we would start the children early and encourage them, along with their parents to exercise and eat right.

Moms and dads, husbands and wives–it really is necessary to look out for each other.

The impossible always takes a little longer than the difficult. First it's always impossible, then it becomes difficult, and with faith, energy and a little more time, **it's done.** If we wrap our minds around the situation, and know it is right, faith and God's providence can move mountains to make a way that, in the beginning, seems impossible. Back to our question, "How can I (or we) get started on a "fitness plan" with no cash to pay for a fitness trainer or join a health club at this present time?"

I shared earlier how, as a child, I was motivated by Jack LaLanne to mimic his moves and, as a high school wrestler, to get into shape and somehow stay fit. As a young adult with few resources, I learned to use what I had to build my body and mind and develop habits. I disciplined myself to keep walking, stretching, working out with homemade weights, and using stress impact on my body between door frames and furniture. I did sit ups, push ups, pull ups, jumping jacks and aerobics to develop specific body areas. I always had a desire to help others and knew I would become a personal fitness trainer early on as a young person.

I got started by training some athletes and other clients right in my apartment. Eventually after lots of word-of-mouth advertising about results my clients enjoyed, I was able to develop a well-equipped professional studio where I now work with many men and women of various ages and backgrounds. This is my twenty-seventh year and I have clients that come year after year and love how they feel and look–strong and healthy.

The moral of this story is never give up! Where there is a will you will find the way. Keep the desired goal as top priority in your thoughts and actions. You will find resources beyond yourself through faith in a God who loves you and wants you to know and trust Him.

I have found as my faith developed through a personal experience with the author of the Bible, that He and His Word are to be taken seriously and trusted. God is not a magic lamp to be rubbed for personal gain. He describes Himself as a loving Father who has given each of us the incredible gift of life with talents to empower us to be blessed and for us to bless others.

A faith based life in God adds a transforming spiritual dimension.

In the Bible, God gives us promises. If we will trust Him and His word our lives can become transformed in every aspect of our lives. He will conform our lives to His likeness.

In the New Testament it says if we use the talents given us, God will bless, enhance and multiply them. If we are careless and undisciplined and do not use them as intended, *we will lose them. Simply, it's use them or lose them!*

My advice is to start where you are, face the situations before you, be realistic and begin changing your circumstances with positive attitudes and actions to accomplish planned goals that benefit you and yours. Most important, get in touch with your Creator. You will find God has great pleasure and joy over those who find and trust Him. This is not intended to be a sermon, just a personal testimony of His presence, power and love that is blessing my life. Obstacles are in the way to help us build purpose, perseverance and persistence into our characters. Like stones on a narrow path, when rolled away, you can move on towards your planned destination. In order to advance in the future, we usually need to evaluate our past actions. Please consider the following challenge to physically profit in the future.

To profit or not to profit? A question that only you can answer

Physically speaking, in the last two years, has your health profited as much as your finances? Please write down your responses to this question below. If you gained weight, write that down as a loss. If you used to work out and stopped, write it down as a loss. If you are leaner now than two years ago, write that down as a profit. If you are exercising more now than before, list it as a profit. Do the same if you are or are not eating healthier now than two years ago. Were your eating habits a profit or loss? What does the overall picture look like? Are you increasing more deposits for health dividends, or depleting your health account?
(I hope this will help you visualize your condition.)

Addictive Habits are prime obstacles to a healthy body

Daily we are bombarded with visual and audio messages that are designed to impact our minds and wills to submit to the cultural lifestyles presented as the norm–encouraging us to join with the cool segment of our society. The advertising agencies have a myriad of ways and means to get into our heads and tickle our fancies. Their impact informs us what to wear, such as Tommy whatever's clothes, drive a Jag, smoke a Virginia Skims and drink lots of Smearenough Vodka with other provocatively cool intellectuals.

Advertising works! When I was young, I remember seeing countless cigarette ads on TV and billboards. Ads like, "I'd walk a mile for a Camel" cigarette, and the rugged cowboy that became the Marlboro Man, sitting high in the saddle while lighting up with a match ignited over his blue jeans. How about the Virginia Slims ad for the ladies? A tall attractive woman with great hair and fine features walks into a room, grabs a pack of Slims, taps the pack, takes one out. She lights up and all is very good; "You've come a long way baby." **Not so good...**ads like these have done much damage to the health of millions of our children, men and women.

Quite frankly, it was images like the Marlboro Man that had me wanting to smoke. That along with the fact that my father smoked, and seeing other boys smoke who also wanted to be like their fathers. I thought when I smoked it made me look more like a man. In my younger years, it seemed to me almost every male Hollywood star I would see had a cigarette hanging out of his mouth. These images stuck with me and started to lead me down the road to physical bankruptcy.

Everywhere we go, we see the media promoting something that is not beneficial for our health. Back in the early 70's, Billie Dee Williams, a popular

African American, used to come on TV promoting Colt 45 malt liquor. There is power–a lot of power–through advertising to impact our minds. Those ads encouraged a very large number of African American men to drink Colt 45.

As a society, we need to be more proactive and use the media to promote more healthy life styles–especially to help our young children, many of whom are overweight and out of physical shape.

After seeing the movie, "The Magnificent Seven, " Yul Brynner became one of my favorite actors. Before his death from lung cancer, Yul video taped a commercial telling people not to smoke. He said he would still be alive today if he had not smoked. I thought, "Wow, we need more ads like that." I would love to see one which reads like this, "I would walk a mile if I could, but because of my smoking, I can barely walk a block. Please don't smoke–for your health's sake."

How about one like this? You see a young looking couple in their sixties running on the beach together saying, "Invest in your health; we did and it's the best investment we ever made."

If it were possible for me, I would bombard the media with ads promoting health and fitness. You would see well known stars on TV turning down alcoholic drinks, openly opting for something healthy instead. If we want to assure our families of a healthy future, we must take steps toward promoting more healthy lifestyles. People are living longer now because of medical advances. But are they living healthier? Let's all do our part to promote the concept of investing in our health.

Gambling, an addictive habit that destroys families and healthy living

Gambling has become epidemic as local and state governments have opted to use lotteries to increase revenue. They have opened the way for the casinos and slots to saturate our society with a *"Get Rich Quick"* mentality. Now with the internet and the open acceptance of gambling, many individuals squander their resources and they and their families suffer the crushing consequences. If this reminds you of someone who is hooked, I suggest you help that one find help with a trained professional. This addiction is as difficult to break as seeking to overcome a drug habit.

You may not be a gambler with cash, but we all have been gamblers at some time in our lives–not in the forms of cash bets placed or in the slots at the casinos or lottery tickets–but with our health.

When we take our health for granted, when we eat foods that are not good for our cardio system or continually overeat more than we should, we are gambling with our lives. If the doctor says we should eat healthier and eat less, and we don't take his advice, then we are gambling with our health. The real issue is how long will we gamble with our health by misusing our bodies? Constant late night binges and a lack of exercise; or any day when we do not invest in our health, is a day spent gambling with our lives, whether we admit it or not. When we carry excess weight around we gamble that we won't have a heart attack, or our blood pressure won't rise.

Yes, we have all, sometimes during our lives, been certified gamblers. The worst thing about gambling with our health is that we can never win. The fruit of neglect is a breakdown, not a breakthrough. The odds are against us if we do not exercise and are careless with our diet. We are heading down the road to physical bankruptcy. I don't care how wealthy you are or how much money you win in the casinos, no one is wealthy enough to gain back their health once it is lost. *If you want to be a winner, don't gamble with your health. Our health is not to be gambled with-neither are the resources given to us to meet our family's needs and bless others.*

Food for Fitness

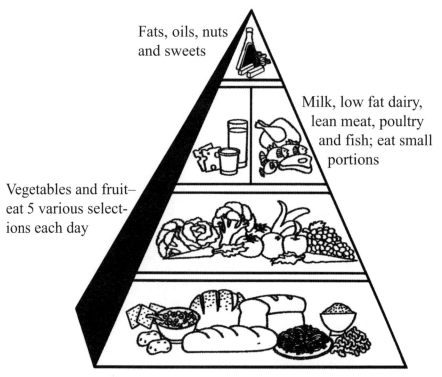

Fats, oils, nuts and sweets

Milk, low fat dairy, lean meat, poultry and fish; eat small portions

Vegetables and fruit– eat 5 various selections each day

Breads, cereals, starchy vegetables like potatoes and beans–eat a variety

The Healthy Food Pyramid for Healthy Bodies

Chapter Four

Preventive Investments

Pay rich dividends

Prevention always costs less, compared with the cost for a cure

It is always a smart investment to pay to prevent a serious problem rather than struggling to fix something that is out of control. When it relates to our health, it is a very wise decision. Neglecting our health can cost more than the physical discomfort; it can cost us cash and lots of it. When was the last time you applied for medical insurance? Do you remember how the rates jump up as time passes?

When you've had prior medical claims, your rates will be generally higher. When diagnosed as being in poor physical condition, or if you smoke, drink, and have high blood pressure, your rates soon reflect this with increases. No company wants to insure anyone who is determined to be a high risk. Being physically fit is like wearing a seat belt before a car crash. No accident was expected, but being prepared saves more than a pound of cure.

Consider cash outlays for health issues that show up when not expected. This happens far less in health conscious families who exercise. It usually will cost a family a lot more to get someone in and out of a hospital than it would to invest in the person's health in a preventive way. The habit of using foresight instead of hindsight is the type of insurance which produces many benefits for peace of mind.

Today, many of the health insurance providers recognize the wisdom of prevention and now offer payment for seniors and disabled people on Medicare for memberships to select health clubs. They bring their senior clients, at no cost to them, into a program called, "The Silver Sneakers Fitness Program." This program includes:

*A basic fitness center membership, at no additional cost, that includes conditioning classes as well as the use of strength tools and swimming.

*The specially-designed, low-impact Silver Sneakers Class, which promotes increased strength, flexibility, balance and coordination with aerobics.

*Special events and health education seminars

Another aspect of this program is called Silver Sneakers Steps. This is a self-directed, pedometer-based physical activity and walking program that allows you to measure progress, track and increase activities. It's a program that provides the equipment, tools and motivation necessary for people to achieve a healthier lifestyle through increased physical activity. Silver Sneakers Steps is for people living fifteen or more miles from a participating fitness center. These programs are available to anyone enrolled in Part B and entitled to Part A of Medicare through age or disability.

Many progressive corporations now provide employee fitness programs.

One of the executives who trains with me and owns a company told me he pays for 200 of his employees to have memberships in health clubs. He believes it is a wise investment. He knows it helps them stay physically and mentally sharp and the company profits through greater efficiency in their performance.

Large companies, like Microsoft, have provided health club benefits for executives for decades. Their executives are in a high performance work environment with a management system that closely monitors individual contributions and progress. They work in a highly competitive atmosphere which takes the executives' continual full performance to keep up with coworkers and company expectations.

U.S. corporations lose billions of dollars through lost man hours over health issues every year. More and more companies of all sizes now provide many incentives and programs to keep their workers mentally and physically fit. It's wise investing which pays back great returns through higher productivity.

I mentioned earlier, one of my clients provide memberships for 200 plus employees to use health and fitness studios. Also, he has ordered 200 copies of this book to be given to each employee to help keep fitness a top priority for workers and their families.

Any corporation would love to see their employees improve and increase their physical assets. As employees increase their overall wellness, generally their work starts to improve along with their health. Mental sharpness improves remarkably when workers are fit.

If you are a member of your employer's management team, here are a few things I would like you to consider. Are your employees draining away company resources with excessive sick days and workers compensation claims? Does employee lack of concern over their health and conditioning eat away at your company's profits with abuse of sick days which raise your insurance premiums? People have talked about this subject for years. Talking alone will not change things.

You have got to get your employees looking at the company's view point. Raises come slower, sales fall off when a company loses their competitive edge, and employees find themselves out looking for another job! It takes teamwork and individual, personal commitment, to keep any company productive and running smoothly and profitable.

One way to motivate your employees is to initiate some type of rewards or incentive program for employees that go three to six or twelve months without using a sick day. Give them recognition before the other employees. Rewards can be small but thoughtful. For those who go a year and beyond, the rewards could be more valuable–like a dinner out with their spouse. Encourage and motivate employees to be a part of a team that is dedicated to keeping physically fit and helping the company grow strong.

For those who can afford it, a company workout facility can pay for itself from benefiting workers to keep fit. Quite honestly, it's a great idea. Healthy employees get sick less, many times not at all. A lot of people talk themselves into becoming sick. They wake up sneezing and the next thing they say, *"I think I'm sick."* Because they project the negative, many do become sick. Or, my favorite is: several people in the company have actually caught the flu bug. They tell everyone else about it. You hear about the stomachs being queasy, noses running, their heads hurting and you, too, immediately think you've caught the flu when you wake up the next morning with your nose running. Guess what happens next; you start to have the symptoms, in fact, you, too, will get sick. If you would have just said, *"My nose is running, yet it's off to work I go,"* you may not have succumbed.

So you see, if you can get a revelation in this area, and take action, you will have the potential to save your company lots of lost work hours, and lots of money. A healthy employee is less likely to get sick and tends to be more alert as well. What kind of an employee are you? One who is physically fit and could reduce injuries at work as well as workers compensation claims? Are you ready for whatever comes next? If you answer *"Yes,"* you are very valuable to your company.

Your body does not need to depreciate like that dollar you hold dear. *The dollar is steadily depreciating* and there is nothing we can do about it. Oh, but our health–that's another story. If we could get a revelation in this area of our lives… we would be on the way to physical solvency. Don't wait till 20/20 does a news special on how to make the body last longer before you start to take care of your health. Seeing is believing. I have worked with many people well into their sixties and early seventies and the way in which their bodies changed from the minute they started training was incredible. My friend John had, literally, no shape. He was straight; no V-shaped back, no visible mass to his shoulders–nothing. John, like so many others that I have trained, could easily testify that his body has appreciated like a fine house in the right location, location, location. Location is what they say when you are looking for a property to invest in. Well if you want the highest *Physical Health Yield* for your time spent on this earth, look in the mirror. You are better than any property that your money could ever afford. So invest, invest, invest. As you keep on investing, you keep appreciating what you have. That dollar you invest today will buy less tomorrow, but the investment you make into your health will yield more than you could ever imagine.

Increase your physical assets while working

Here is an opportunity to keep moving and stretching while on the phone. If you have a sit-down job and talk a lot on the phone, make sure you use a cordless that gives you the opportunity to stand and talk. For starters, I recommend that every other time the phone rings, stand up and talk.

Now you are open for a mini-workout. People with standing jobs tend to burn more calories than someone in a sitting job. If it is going to be a long conversation, start marching in place behind your desk or cubicle while you talk. Pick up your legs and keep them moving. Once you start picking up those legs, you'll find it harder than you thought. Also switch the phone every other minute from one side to the other and use the phone as a tool to do a neck stretch. When you do that you are doing what I like to call the "*looking stretch,*" in the workout section of this book.

Automated asset building exercises

Remember, when starting out, to perform all exercises in the order listed, in the Invest in Your Health Exercise Plan. If, at anytime, you are performing these exercises you feel any discomfort, I suggest you stop immediately. Wait until the discomfort leaves, then move on to the next exercise–taking note of the movement or exercise you may feel caused the discomfort. Many times when someone has not worked out for a while, their bodies will tend to be sensitive to anything they do that's different. That is why it is so important to start slowly and take it easy. After a couple of weeks of physical conditioning and training, try the exercise that caused the discomfort again, If it still does not feel good in your body, then it is probably not a good exercise for you. It should not be done again. Quite honestly, there are exercises that people do with the best form in the world, but for some reason the exercise causes pain or discomfort and we don't always know why. So, leave it alone. If it doesn't feel right don't do it. The Invest in Your Health plan is intentionally designed to make you feel like you're not doing anything until finally you are into the habit of exercising. As you get into the habit, the intensity of your training will increase and your body will actually start to crave the workouts.

In order for you to get the most out of your time invested, read the underlined part over to yourself, at least three times!

"I believe in quality, not quantity. When I am exercising I will concentrate on all aspects of the movement, the contraction phase, and the lengthening phase. I will never sacrifice my form just to get another repetition completed. The way I start an exercise, is the way I will finish the exercise.

I can tell you with all honesty and sincerity I have never had a client of mine injured when they were working out with me, and I know without a doubt, it is because they focused on what they were doing. I never allowed them to do an exercise incorrectly just so they could feel like they got that extra repetition in.

The smartest investment you'll ever make is in your health.

You've invested in an IRA.

You save money for your children's college tuition.

You invest monthly in a life insurance plan.

You spend hundreds of dollars a year for medical insurance.

You pay monthly premiums for home owners insurance.

You even spend money monthly to protect your car with insurance.

And some of you even save 10% of your income for your church (and that's a good thing).

But do we allow even 4% of our time to promote better health and fitness? Imagine where you would be physically if you took 4% of your time in a sixteen hour day, three days a week and dedicated it to improving your own health.

Most of us spend very little time on our health. Yes, we take vacations but come back too stressed out for our jobs.

Or we can spend more money later for hospital and doctor bills.

For sure…the best, and smartest investment we can make will always be *our health*.

Time for others, but not for yourself

A friend and client of mine, Peter Kelsey, whom I have personally trained for three years now, asked me this question, "If your best friend was on his death bed, and you knew he was going to die soon, would you drive an hour and a half just to visit him?" I said, "Of course I would, wouldn't you?" He then said, "Yes I would also. The reason I'm asking you this is that all of us eventually will die, but most people are too busy trying to make a buck to even put in thirty minutes, three times a week, for their own health." Which really makes sense when you think about it. "Is it not wiser to put the time in now while we are reasonably healthy, than wait until we are in the hospital thinking of what we should have done?" We take time for our friends, our employers, but no time for ourselves. What's wrong with this picture? Think about it! Think hard!

The importance of laughter and smiles–hidden dividends

Doctors have stated that fifteen minutes of laughing, is equivalent to five minutes of moderate jogging.

Have you ever wondered why you are out of breath when you have been laughing hard? It's because laughing can be somewhat of an aerobic workout when you do it long enough.

Treat laughter the way you do drinking water. Get as much in as you can.

One of the first things I want to tell you is to surround yourself with people who love to laugh. Laugh with them and it will have a positive effect on your life.

When they say a smile is worth its weight in gold, that is exactly what they mean.

A smile can make a person's day.

Have you ever felt a little down and someone walked by and smiled as they said hello?

It has been known for quite a while that sick people who laugh tend to recover more quickly.

Smiling makes a person look younger.

Tips to cutting employer health care costs

Corporate fitness programs: Healthier employees are generally more productive employees because healthier employees tend to be better producers. For years, companies like General Electric have been having team building sessions that last anywhere from one to two days. They do this to teach people the importance of the team. No man is an island. Companies that are successful, generally are so because their people work as a team and are committed to the company's growth and success.

Several years ago, I can remember being asked to be a team leader at one of the team training sessions for a company. I was delighted to help knowing we were doing something that would actually help the people become more productive for their company. If your company leaders are thinking about having a team building session I would like to encourage them to e-mail me at ron@FitnessKing.com or call me at 1.877.fit.king and allow me the opportunity to talk about your company's health needs and team building skills. I use new and creative team building exercises to help motivate employees to take better care of themselves and help them to really work as a team and strengthen the company.

Have quarterly meetings: meetings that are geared to inspire employees to take better care of themselves. In these meetings you will provide a motivational speaker to encourage good health and acknowledge those who have not lost any days being ill.

Start an awards program: For those who have had no sick days off, acknowledge their accomplishment. Award people for their healthy life style. It will not only motivate them to use less sick days, it will help develop a sense of pride, in the fact that they don't get sick.

Have an awards banquet: Hand out awards for the people who have less or no sick days each year. Also incorporate a volunteer steps program making sure to first talk with a few people who are avid walkers and a few who are not. You want to try to get as many people as possible to become walkers in their off-time from work. Walking on a regular basis can lower blood pressure, reduce overeaters' weight, and even cure some Type 2 adult diabetes. Try and get people to team up in specific departments. You can hand out Certificates of Award to those who have accomplished specific goals to reinforce strong, healthy attitudes for good health.

What does it mean to *you* to be healthy?

"What does it mean to be healthy, to exercise and take care of my body? Every newsstand and book store is filled with health and fitness books and magazines. I have always tried to choose the right foods, exercise and try to read articles on health and fitness. I am now a health and fitness junkie. I like to focus on my health as I am getting older. I recognize that the key to living longer is to stay exercising and carefully watch the foods that I eat. Many of my friends do not exercise or eat right for good health. Many eat too much at one time. Some have health issues and are on medications. My personal appearance is important to me and my goal is to stay healthy and fit.

About a year ago a very special friend generously gave me ten personal training sessions with, 'The Fitness King' (Ron Henderson) for my birthday. All I could think about was that this gift was too extravagant. How will I ever be able to continue after the ten sessions? Is this something I really want to do? I finished the ten sessions and continued another eight weeks. It was good to go one-on-one as it made me focus on the technique for each muscle group. I continued to move on with the good information I learned. Each week, I go to a local gym four or five times per week. It clears my mind of the stress from every day living.

I do miss the one-on-one sessions and maybe someday I can go back to 'The Fitness King.' I plan to stay focused as it has become my way of life."
Anonymous

Chapter Five

Physically Healthy?

What's it really like to be Physically Healthy?

First, it feels good. It's good when you know that what you know is good! Like everything else, there are levels of health. It takes a lot of commitment to become and stay healthy. Once you have obtained a level of physical fitness, keep pressing on. It is a lifestyle that is obtained by lots of hard work. I've found there are six basic ingredients to staying healthy, and it is up to each of us.

Commitment: We need to make exercise a priority in our lives by taking time out for ourselves to do something, physically, on a consistent basis. We must add, also, our unintentional exercises like those found in the automatic extras section of this book.

If you have trouble staying committed, remember what you sow, you will reap. Taking care of our health is the same as taking care of those investments we have. If we only invest in them when we want, then our return will not be as great. And our health is no different. You rarely see a man or woman who is in top physical shape, who just works out when they want. No, these people workout regularly and are committed to keeping their health goals.

We, too, must stay committed to our health and work out regularly if we want to reap the positive benefits and obtain physical independence. Who knows, maybe some day they will be included in the marriage vows: I promise to take care of myself to the best of my abilities as long as I shall live. When I was young and watched the TV show, "Star Trek," I always liked when Dr. Spock would say, "Live long and prosper." Now, I may be stepping on a few toes with this statement but I don't think the prospering part of his famous saying had anything to do with prospering financially. I think it had more to do with a healthy and full life. This is what I want you to get from this book: the real importance of taking care of ourselves early on in our lives and until death do we part.

Ownership: We need to take ownership. We need to be responsible. First, we must make a decision to limit our fast food pick-ups, and our fat foods consumed. Remember when we eat something that we really don't want, we are no longer in control, the food is! I'm not saying we can't eat at a fast food restaurant, because we both know some times it just can't be helped. There are times when we just can't avoid it. Make better food choices when we can. We need to commit, be more responsible and take ownership. There are times when we may want to splurge on some salty or greasy foods. It may not be the best choice, but your health will not be greatly affected by it in moderation.

I believe that we can, in fact, eat whatever we want as long as we are not eating whatever we want, all the time. It's about moderation. We must stay in control of how and what we choose to eat. We need to be consuming what is better for us from a nutritional standpoint. So, as we begin our journey toward physical independence let us not forget it's our bodies and our health. We decide how we want to function–what we put into our bodies and what we do with them.

Management: Take the manager role. Determine to be a leader, not a follower. Don't sit at the bar, with your friends, drinking alcohol and consuming one fatty appetizer after another if you don't really want to. You see, it is easy to get deterred from your healthy lifestyle, although most of us probably don't believe it. There are lots of people who actually will get jealous when they see you looking better. Some of them might even be your friends. It is not that they are out to get you. It is probably more a feeling of guilt because of their lack of concern over the condition of their own bodies. Sometimes, people will even try to bait us by eating certain foods that they know we like, with the hope that they might be able to tempt us off our regimen of healthy living.

When those times arrive we will have to be a leader and boldly say, "No thanks!" Those invitations come filled with useless calories that can be a detriment to our health. Remember, its all about loading up our health assets column and lowering our health liabilities column. A good investment manager is always aware of where they are financially. We need to be aware and in control of where we are health wise. We can do this if we take charge and manage our health.

Money: Make money second or third, or anything else but first, in your life! And remember I am not saying don't strive for it. We all need it. What I am saying is keep it in its proper place. As long as you have good health you can earn more money. I recently went on the internet and looked up wealthy people who committed suicide. It was shocking in some regards. In other ways somewhat understandable. These people had the money, but no health and no God, and therefore had no peace. Yes, money can buy almost everything, but good health, peace of mind, and happiness. Only God can provide those. Also, replace the phrase, "he that has the money makes the rules," with "he that has his health, lives longer and defines the rules." I remember hearing a song when I was in high school, I believe it was called, 'For the Love of Money.' It talked about what people will do for money, and how important it is. A distinctive line in the song said people will sell their soul just to get it. I even had a former client of mine say, "It's all about the money; nothing else really maters." For this gentleman, nothing else did matter and therefore nothing but money was ever manifested in his life. He was always depressed, and lonely which explained his weekly trips to his psychologist. Yes, that was one man who put money first and reaped the financial rewards of that decision. He ended by sacrificing his mental and physical health in the process. Remember whatever is at the top of the list is where you focus the most. Whatever is at the bottom is where you focus the least.

I've said it before and I'll say it again, my personal priorities are spiritual fitness, physical fitness and financial fitness, and I have peace in my heart. Ever since I have made spiritual fitness first in my life, I have never been happier. At age fifty-two, I have never felt better physically in my life. As I end this segment, I implore you to not make money first in your life.

Independence: Physical independence–think about it! Work toward it! Obtain it! Physical independence can be yours. Approach your health with the latter years in mind. The next time you go to the local mall, start observing people. You will notice the majority are either overweight or walking around as if they have no energy. Now try observing people who you think are close to your age. Do they have an energetic walk? Are they walking tall? Or are they bent over and moving slowly? Every time I see someone close to my age moving slowly and out of shape, it makes it even more clear in my mind why I need to stay in shape. I stay in shape with a consistent exercise program. You see, I want to walk tall like Jack LaLanne who still does push-ups like Jack Palance did on national TV. My dad, at age eighty would put most young men to shame with his energy and physical stature. Pound for pound he has had less body fat than people I've just mentioned. It is because of his consistent workouts over many years.

If the negative images don't motivate you to do something about your long term health, and physical independence, maybe the positive images will. Find a role model with a good energy level that is older than you or your age and imagine yourself being fit in your later years. Continue to work toward your physical independence. **If you want it, you can achieve it.**

Time Management: Now that you are aware of how the time management tool can help you, make a decision to use it. Time, remember, is the one thing in life that cannot be replaced. Once it is used, it is through. We can't magically reverse the clock, but we can slow it down. Once we get into reasonable shape, we find ourselves needing less rest and having more energy. We can do more in a shorter time without wearing out. This is good as it becomes easier to keep a schedule for your workouts once you've moved your priorities around to go for health over wealth. Time management is the sixth and final key to getting it and keeping it all together.

The above six portions of the "6 Steps to Manage Your Health" lay out an overall plan to help you get strong and stay strong and healthy on into your later years. Give it your best effort to keep your health and stamina up, vital, rich and full.

Television ads may promise the impossible.

"Lose ten pounds in ten days." All you have to do is order the product and find out thirty days later that you haven't lost five pounds yet, let alone ten pounds. Well, we live in a microwave society where everyone is looking for an overnight cure-all. We want our results to be here quickly and with ease, like how about NOW. Some of us want to lose weight so badly that we'll even risk surgery to shorten our stomachs. Yes, it is like investing in the stock market. If we hear that a stock is doing well, we want to have some. We buy some, even though we really don't know if it is good or not. If it doesn't do well, we'll sell it and buy another stock that may not be so hot either. We'll keep buying and selling stocks hoping that the next one will make us rich. We've all heard the term, "bullish, " in the stock market. Well, I want you to get "bullish" over your health while you can.

Right now the advantages to invest in your health far surpass any and all of the monetary investments you have ever made. Remember growing up and hearing your parents make the comment, "You don't get something for nothing."? That holds true today and will do so always. This is as true as "anything worth having, is worth working for." The amazing thing about my program is the way it helps you to develop good exercise habits. You can get started at the level you can handle with ease and move toward your personal goals.

A poem for your thoughts

Time, oh, time, where did it go?
From board room to lunch meetings
I had to go.
I've been given a raise
So I have no choice,
With the extra money
I can buy a Rolls Royce,

From lunch to the stockbroker
I must go;
I've got to find out if my stocks
Are high or low
Yes, money means a lot to me
From fur coats to diamond rings,
Heaven knows,
I need these things.

Whether we are rich
or poor
We all have to choose
Whether to open that door;
The door to great health or
The door to great wealth–
Which one will it be?
You choose for you
And I'll choose for me!

(Ron Henderson)

Seven keys to physical independence
Key No. 1

Knowing Your Physical Condition — The first key is one of the most important. Knowing where you are health wise will help you see the real importance of making the necessary changes to come to your full potential. Write down in the lines provided, exactly what your physical state is at this time of your life. Please list all injuries, ailments, weight problems, or anything that could affect what you would like to do to improve your health.

My Present Physical Condition

_____
_____
_____
_____
_____
_____
_____
_____
_____
_____

Now that you are clear where you are physically, what would you like to do to change your current circumstances? The next part is Key No. 2 which will give an accounting of what exactly you want to accomplish and how you plan to get it done. I call it the Re-firing Plan.

A Re-Firement Plan
Key No. 2
The Best Retirement—You see, I don't believe in retiring, I believe in _re-firing_. Join me in my plan for going into those later years of life, ignited, excited and prepared physically. I plan to go into it full throttle. How do you plan to live your late years? On this next sheet, write down your own plan. Writing your thoughts down will help get the information embedded into your subconscious where it can strengthen your will to proceed to meet your physical goals.

My Wants

_____
_____
_____
_____
_____
_____
_____

My plan to accomplish it

_____
_____
_____
_____
_____
_____

Key No. 3

Words — Eliminate many negatives out of your vocabulary. Statements like "I always get sick," will merely cultivate the ground for sickness and disease to enter into your body. When you wake up in the morning with a cough do you automatically say, "I must be coming down with a cold." If you say that or anything closely related, you are a candidate for frequent colds because your words are sowing the seeds.

Eliminate statements like these: "I can't control my appetite." Or, "I've always been this way, I don't have time to exercise." Phrases like these can go a long way in keeping you from getting to your goals. If you want to change the harvest, you merely have to change the seeds you plant. I call this the positive seeds of sowing your words.

See what a difference it will make toward progression of your physical independence. Speaking life into your circumstances will build you up physically, spiritually, and mentally. Words like, "I find it easy to control my appetite." Or statements like, "I always make time to get my exercise in." Life and death are in the power of the tongue. We can use it for our benefit or to our harm. The choice is always ours. As we keep speaking the positive, our good seeds continue to grow.

Key No. 4

Mind — Eliminate as many negative thoughts as you possibly can. When you think negatively, you sow the negative seeds with your mind. Don't think the worst for your situation. Think positive. Think on things that are pure and just–things that are bright and beautiful. What you put in your mind comes out the same way. Start thinking of what you will feel like once you get into shape. Also, think of what you will look like. See yourself having more energy and running with the kids. As you know, in the financial world, if you file for bankruptcy, it will take you several years to get your credit reestablished. With our bodies, it will take some time, as well. But the time it takes to physically build up your physical credit score, shortens when you practice all of the seven keys that you are learning right now.

Key No. 5

Body — Eliminate as many negative habits as you can. This will take a little time because of all the areas needing work. Changing is the hardest for many. It takes a lot to change the physical part, the actual doing of something. Yes, if you are constantly overeating beyond what your body was designed for and thereby taxing your heart–and causing additional strain on your joints and ligaments– you will need to change. You will need to control the habit of overeating. You cannot continue to disrespect your body without reaping negative consequences.

How do we sow the positive? Well for starters, we want to make sure that we take our time and start slowly with whatever we do, so we do not injure our bodies. I recommend that you start slowly and easily until your body becomes stronger and can do more.

Key No. 6

Accountability — The accountability key means exactly what it says. It is very important to make a commitment to an accountability partner. To mentally change a direction many times is not easy. You must pick someone who will definitely hold you accountable. This person could be your spouse, a close friend, or another family member. Please don't forget to write down your commitment to exercise on the Physical Bankruptcy Accountability form. Remember to start slowly and to take your time. You didn't get where you are overnight. But it won't take a lifetime to change either. So be patient, be consistent, and speak life to your situation with your mind, work and body.

Key No. 7

Share Your Keys — The last key, No. 7, is probably the most important of all the keys. This one teaches you to share all the keys you've learned with seven other people you know. Each time you share your keys with another person, you are increasing your chances of being able to stay debt free. Each time you repeat what you have learned, it serves as a strong reinforcement and can go a long way in helping you achieve physical independence and get out of physical bankruptcy. At the same time, you are helping your fellow man to live a healthier and, possibly, a longer life.

I have also learned over the years that if you want something in life then you must give the very thing that you want to someone else. If you are seeking to improve your health and get out of bankruptcy, help another; share what you have learned.

The Seven Names: At this time take a few minutes and think about with whom you would like to share the information on the seven keys. Write down seven names.

_____

_____

_____

_____

_____

_____

_____

_____

_____

_____

Start them out early: The phrase, "Train up a child in the way he should go and when he is old, he will not depart from it," is in the book of Proverbs. It is just as much true today as the day it was recorded. Our children do whatever they do on the basis of what they hear and see. You would not dream that your children would be saying curse words. They merely are speaking words they have heard on the radio, TV or some other person speaking. We, alone, are in charge of our children's behavior, fitness and health. When you exercise, let your children watch you. They will try to copy your actions. Ladies, remember when your daughters were young, and they used to go into your closet and try out your shoes, and put on your make-up? It is instinctive the way they watch you do what you do and then they want to do the same things. They want to be like their mommy and daddy.

The parental influence

I remember my father was visiting me at my workout studio in Minneapolis. I jokingly said to my dad, "Get up on those two bars and see how long you can hold your legs straight out in front of you." My dad looked at me and said, "Why, is that supposed to be hard?" I remarked, "I just want to see if you can do it." My father positioned himself on the two bars and proceeded to raise his legs straight out into a perfect L position as any gymnast could. I have to admit that I was pretty impressed when my father got off the bars because he was able to hold his legs straight out for almost forty seconds. It was amazing to watch because most people under the age of thirty would be doing well if they could hold their legs up for thirty seconds.

Yes, I am fortunate to have had parents who believed in exercise. My father works out with the weights two to three times a week and rides the stationary bike at least three days a week. Wait, there is more. He also is still able to do at least two sets of pull-ups and does at least thirteen to fifteen reps, and on a good day, he will do three sets of fifteen reps in his workouts. My dad is a great example to me on how exercise can enhance your physical life.

When you see my father walking, you would think he is on a mission–he walks so fast. Yes, my dad still moves like someone in their early thirties, and I do not say that to brag; I say it because it is the truth. Dad stopped working years ago. But he didn't stop working out.

I have always hated the word retire. When I look at the word, it makes me think of shutting down, to quit, to go to sleep. I prefer the word, refire, to ignite, to inspire, to renew. It is great to see my father has done his assignment and has prepared himself physically for the later years of life.

You feel like a rocket ship ready to explore new territories, new horizons, and you'll have the energy to do it. My desire for you is that you not only take this journey but that you would encourage your children to follow by your example. At the end of a book I am currently writing for children, I have a song that I wrote for my kids and it goes like this: "I know I can't sit, so I'll have to stay fit so I'll run around on a turn table. I know what it takes, so a promise I will make is to continue as long as I'm able."

My friend, you don't have to stay physically bankrupt. You can get started and live a fuller life if you start and stay on a consistent exercise program geared towards physical independence. My desire for you is that you not only recognize these truths but you act upon them for you and your family and continue as long as you are able.

Plan your child's succeeding for a better success rate

When it comes to our children's future, what are we planning for? When I'm asking about planning, I mean, in what are we investing our time and energy? Is it our children's college education? If it is, we better start saving early on. We will need to make some firm commitments if we want to be prepared to help our children with their future college educations. If you are hoping that maybe the fairy godmother will wave her magic wand and "Presto," four years of college education paid for…keep hoping! Most of us will have to discipline ourselves to save. How well we invest and save will not only determine where we are financially, as far as college is concerned, but will also affect everything we do in life that we deem important.

Now maybe you're one of those fortunate people not concerned for college money for your children. You already have more than you need. Your biggest concern is to figure out what are the best stocks in which you can invest. When your children do grow up, their nest egg for college will be waiting for them. That's great! Let me remind you, whatever you planned for your children, from an investment point of view, will not be worth its weight in pennies–let alone gold–if you haven't invested in your children's health.

Many people like me also invest into their children's spiritual health by bringing them into a God–centered environment like a church or synagogue on a weekly basis. We do that because we know the importance of our children having and knowing God in their lives. We want them to succeed spiritually speaking, so like finances and their health, we take time to invest.

When you are through reading this book, take time to map out a plan for your whole family. I assure you it is one investment that you'll be glad you took time to invest in. If we don't invest in our families, who will?

Getting out of physical bankruptcy–it's a family affair

Working out should not be just an individual commitment. It's a family necessity. When you start thinking about getting into shape, you quickly realize that it is not just an event but a lifestyle. If you or a family member decides to start a workout program, it will be important that you do it for yourselves, not for someone else. Too many times we find ourselves trying to impress someone–working out two or three days a week before going to a wedding or a class reunion–only to find ourselves quitting once the event is over. Take the step right now to get your body in the best shape of your life, and keep it that way. Stop making New Year's resolutions! Become resolute! You are the only one you need to impress.

We can't determine a family member's life span, or our own, but we can decide the quality level our physical lives can enjoy. Most people prepare financially for their family's present and future needs. Most people have been taught that money makes the world go around. The more money you can make and save for yourself and your family the greater your financial stability will be.

So, the majority of us spend our lives chasing after money, which we deposit into banks only to take out later to invest into stocks, bonds, life insurance policies, and our children's college education. And that's a good thing. What about investing in our children's physical education and health? Are we doing that? If not, why not? We need to be proactive in getting our kids moving and investing into their own physical independence and good health habits. If we don't plan for the family's future, the outcome will be our responsibility. Are you starting to realize the importance of your role? To say it plain and simple, it is never too late to invest into your family's health, or your own personal fitness. Any time is better than no time at all! Of course, it is better to get started early in your life. If you are older, take charge now. You can still slow down the aging process if you just start where you are and keep on going!

My family is financially secure

All through this book you have read about people seeking and obtaining financial independence versus people seeking physical independence. What about your family? Have you planned for your family's physical independence? Are your children out of shape and overweight? You better believe that you had something to do with it, either intentionally or unintentionally. Are your children being raised in an environment that is fitness conscious? As parents, we have the responsibility not only to teach our children how to read and write but to teach them the facts of life so they can enrich and extend their lives. Their personal exercise is the best way to do that for them. This, my friend, is not just taught by word of mouth, but by example. When your children watch you work around the house, see you eat the right foods, walk and exercise, your example will be an encouragement for them to pick up on the things you do.

How many times have you heard a parent say, "I'll have to pinch and save my dollars, if I'm going to help my children get through college." Ask them why they do not have their children work their way through college. The most common response is, "My parents paid my way through college and I don't want my kids to worry how they are going to have time to work and study at the same time. I want them to be focused on their studies without distractions." Whether right or wrong, we to have to think about our children's personal health habits, as well as their formal education. We need to be setting good examples of what it means to be physically fit. I'm not saying we should not work at expanding our financial solvency. That would be a foolish mistake. What I am saying is, we need to know our priorities and then go for it. So what, if our family is financially secure, and we've neglected our family's health?

Chapter Seven

Let's Workout

An easy to follow workout program

In starting this program it will seem as though you are almost doing nothing. This program is designed that way intentionally. Many people begin their exercise programs strong and do too much to begin with. They expect too much to soon. We see this every year with the coming of the New Year's resolutions. Almost all the quality health clubs are packed with hungry people looking to boost their health dividends. Within a few months they are back to their old lifestyle–to their lives, and finances, and forgetting about their health.

This is similar to people who have never saved money before and they start putting so much money in their investment accounts, they run short in other areas. After a couple of calls from creditors, many soon quit putting money into saving accounts, and other financial vehicles, in order to have funds to pay their other obligations.

In fact, I can remember going to an investment seminar that got me so pumped, I opened up a couple of investment accounts, put money into them that I could not afford to do at that time. I became cash strapped, so I eventually closed those accounts. I am sharing this with you to give you my reasons for designing an exercise program in a way to empower you to develop the habits, to do the exercises, without ever joining a gym, or spending another dollar. You can and will be successful with the few dollars you've already invested in this book, if you start slowly and follow the program faithfully.

If I had just kept myself relaxed and consistently putting a small investment into one of those accounts–I still would have been investing, and my wife and I would have a healthy nest egg by now. I started too fast, and put too much into it, and eventually had to quit, too soon.

This is the way people start their exercise program; seeking to move too fast, instead of finding a groove that works, and stay with it consistently. Are you a total novice, or have you been in good shape for a long time? Start slowly and go through the program the way it is designed. Get your body feeling something that is good for it. Once the habit is formed, you can proceed to become a healthy leader within your family.

Remember when you, or someone you know, started smoking cigarettes? No one starts out smoking a pack a day, although it may not take long to get there for some. Everyone starts out with a cigarette or two or three the first day. Eventually they get hooked on something that will destroy their health and automatically go into a pack or more each day.

"I want you to become addicted to working with all the exercises for you own good health! I want you and those around you addicted to something that will improve and keep your health consistent all the days that God gives you life. Remember, the rewards are to the consistent, those who persevere and are resolute." Now that I've said that, here is how you can get started.

It is always better for you to warm-up with a walk or a short bike ride before your exercise workout gets started. It's important to stretch before you start working your muscles and joints. For the most part, these exercises will be done without a proper warm-up. Once these automated exercises are put into practice, you should be ready to do any exercise in this book on a minute's notice. This program is designed to make you more conscious of your various muscles and to think about feeling them, as you move about. Think about your health program the same way you think about your finances–carefully.

First, you will pick three days each week in which you will go through the body toning exercises, or consistently every other day for a total of four days each week. Starting out on week one, you will choose and perform one exercise with ten repetitions every other hour for a different muscle group each time. The time on each exercise will just take a few minutes out of each hour.

So, for the first week you patiently will learn how all the exercises work, taking a new choice for a different part of the body, each time you choose one. Many men especially will seek to work their arms a little more than other body parts and find themselves out of balance physique wise. For the sake of completing the program for all around symmetry, please, everyone must let go of their egos. Men, let's each work toward taking care of our whole body. For the first three months, at the end of each session, record each exercise you completed. This will help you to look back to chart your progress. Each of us will have preferences with the different exercises. Though tempting, keep going on to the next one.

As an example, you could pick an exercise from one of the groups, say, Pushups, as your choice for that hour–out of the chest building group–and complete ten repetitions. Then after an hour's rest, you could choose squats from the leg group as your next exercise that day and do the ten repetitions. After the next hour of doing whatever you need to do or just resting, pick the next one from another muscle group.

On week two, you can pick two exercises from two different groups each hour you workout. Take an hour off and then pick two more for two more different muscle groups. Continue through week two with every other day off. Continue to add another exercise from a different group each week; do three exercises each hour, the third week, four each hour, the fourth week. Continue adding another exercise for the fifth week. During the sixth week, you will be doing six different exercises each hour of your workout, with an hour off between the workout hours.

Remember, I asked you to record your exercises on a daily basis for the first three months? Again I remind you it is truly important for you to put it all together after the first three months. Take some snapshots of yourself before you start and some at the end of your first three months and compare improvement with your exercise record. You will enjoy your position and want to keep on going with these exercises, well managed, at the end of three months. Like your bank account, it will help you keep both your checking and your physical checking account in balance the way your bank book balance helps keep your finances up to date.

Your fitness increases your ability to ward off serious, costly health problems.

Recent medical studies again prove that your personal fitness will help keep you from serious health problems. Trimming down our bodies from a few excessive pounds, and doing light exercise is a major way to take down our high blood pressure.

A recent west coast study by Kaiser Permanente's Center was reported on April 14, 2006 in USA Today. This and other studies show, "healthy lifestyle changes can have a positive impact on risk policies and people will benefit in so many ways," says William Vollmer, co-author of the study. This article pointed out that people walking an average of thirty minutes a day cut their risk of getting diabetes by 58%. It's worth the effort to avoid it!

Other good news shows that cholesterol is not the only health problem impacted by exercise and healthy habits. Diabetes and high blood pressure respond to exercise and a good diet also. The bad news is that there are also many people predisposed to the above problems and will need medication no matter what else is going on.

Power exercises that work 30 muscle groups

The next thirty pages will lay out a different exercise on each page. These are taken from Ron Henderson's Fitness King collection of unique products for your personal health care. These exercises are found in Ron's Fitness + Faith Power Cards. You can use this book which has all the exercises, but not the biblical references.

Our Fitness and Faith Power Cards were created to assist in developing physical and spiritual growth. Each card contains an exercise that works a different muscle group. This program is designed to shape and tone your entire body by following the detailed instructions and illustrations of thirty unique exercises. These exercises are easy to use while watching TV, listening to music or any time. You can purchase a set of The Fitness and Faith Power Cards through my web site: www.fitnessking.com

Exercise No. 1
MARCHING OR RUNNING IN PLACE
Cardiovascular

March or run in place lightly with your feet barely coming off the ground, moving at a pace that's comfortable for you.

Beginners: 30-60 seconds
Intermediates: 60-90 seconds
Advanced: 2-3 minutes

Exercise No. 2

JUMPING ROPE IN PLACE
Cardiovascular

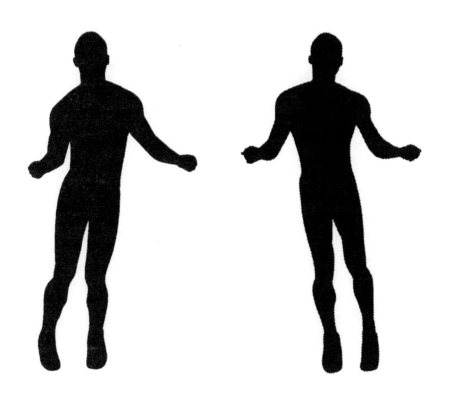

No jump rope is required. Stand with feet about 8" apart, elbows at waist level and bent. Mimic the movement of jumping rope. Keep your steps light and feet close to the ground. You may jump with both feet close to the ground. You may jump with both feet together or you may alternate your feet.

Beginners: 20-30 seconds
Intermediate: 60-90 seconds
Advanced: 1-2 minutes

Exercise No. 3

DANCING SOLO
Cardiovascular

Beginners: dance any style for 60 seconds
Intermediates: 60-90 seconds
Advanced: 2 minutes

Exercise No. 4

CALF RAISES
Gastrocnemius/Soleus

Lying on the floor, raise up on your toes as far as you can, flexing your calf muscles. Hold briefly, then lower. Repeat for ten repetitions.

Exercise No. 5

LEG CURLS
Biceps Femoris/Glutes

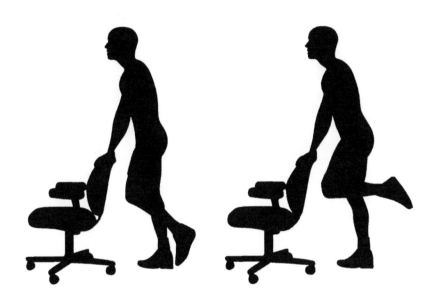

Standing behind a chair, hold the back with both hands. Curl your left leg
up toward the buttocks, making sure to contract your back leg muscles, then
lower leg. Repeat for ten repetitions.

Exercise No. 6

SQUATS
Quadriceps

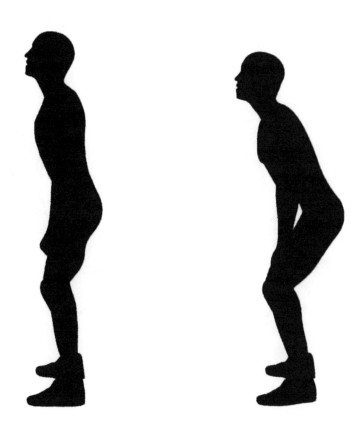

Stand with feet about shoulder width apart. Bend your knees slightly and lower your body about half of the way down and slowly push back up to the starting position. Be sure to keep your head back and your back straight. Remember to contract your quadriceps and glute muscles on the way up. Repeat for ten repetitions.

Exercise No. 7

SIDE LEG LIFTS
Outer Thighs

Lying on your left side with your lower leg bent, lift your right leg as high as possible without straining your leg, and then back down for ten repetitions. Lay on right side and lift leg for ten repetitions.

Exercise No. 8

SIDE BENDS
Obliques

Standing with your feet spread apart, with your hands at your side, keeping the hips stationary, slowly lean to the right and then to the left, concentrating on tightening up the oblique and abdominal muscles. Remember to lean as far to each side as possible without straining the muscles. Stretch one side of muscle while contracting the other. Lean to the right and left for a total of twenty repetitions.

Exercise No. 9

STOMACH CRUNCH
Rectus Abdominis/Upper Abdominis

Lying flat on your back with both legs bent and feet on the floor, place your hands behind your head or cross them over your chest. From this position raise your head half way off the floor and draw your shoulders toward your lower pelvic area, making sure to contract your stomach muscles before returning back to the floor. Complete ten repetitions. Remember to exhale on the way up and to breathe in on the way down. It is very important that you contract your muscles as tight as you can, to increase the intensity of the muscle being worked. Warning! Do not pull on your head or neck as this could strain your cervical vertebra.

SIDE CRUNCHES
Abdominals/Oblique

Lying flat on your back with both legs bent, place the left leg on top of the right knee, put your right hand behind your head, begin to lift your shoulders up and try to touch your left knee with your right shoulder. Be sure to make contact at the top, then return back to the starting position. Remember to try to keep your elbow back, and your knee turned to the outside. Use your hands as support for your head and neck. Do not pull on your neck. Remember to squeeze those abdominal muscles tightly to maximize the contraction. Complete ten repetitions on each side.

Exercise No. 11

TOE TOUCHING CRUNCHES
Upper Abdominal

Lying flat on your back with both legs up in the air, raise head slightly off floor, extend your arms reaching for your toes and bring arms back down. Lower your head, but do not touch the floor. Do a total of ten repetitions. Remember to contract your abdominal as you are reaching upward.

Exercise No. 12

REVERSE CRUNCH
Rectus Abdominis/Lower Abdominals

Lying flat on the floor, with both hands slightly under your buttocks, draw your knees toward your chest and hold. Complete ten repetitions. Remember, do not swing your knees toward your chest, but concentrate on using your lower stomach muscles to pull your knees toward your chest. Remember to breathe out as your knees are being drawn in and breathe out as you lower your knees.

STOMACH FLEX
Loser/Middle/Upper Abdominals

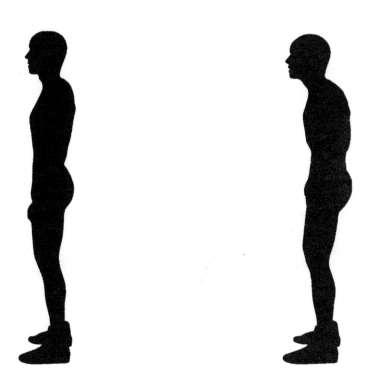

Standing with knees bent slightly, pull your stomach muscles in and hold for ten seconds then relax for five seconds. Complete three repetitions.

Exercise No. 14

LEG PULL-INS
Rectus Abdominis

Sitting on the floor with your hands behind you, lift both feet off the floor and draw your legs in toward your chest, and hold for a brief second making sure to flex your stomach muscles. Then return to the starting position. Complete ten repetitions. Warning! If you feel any strain to your back, discontinue this exercise.

Exercise No. 15

SEATED ABDOMINAL CURL
Pectus Abdominis

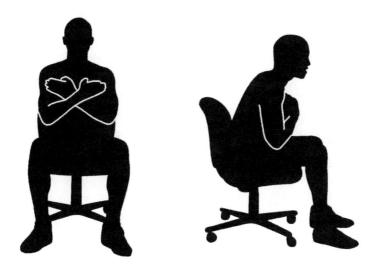

Sit on a chair in an upright position. Cross your arms over your chest, bending at the waist until you feel your abdominal muscles tightening up, then return to up position. Note: Try to keep your abdominals tight when performing this exercise. Complete ten repetitions.

Exercise No. 16

STANDING TWIST
Obliques

Standing with both hands on hips, twist slowly to the right then to the left, making sure to contract your obliques as you twist in each direction for a total of twenty repetitions. Keep your head facing forward.

SIDE LEG PULL-INS
Obliques/Abdominals

Lean on your left side with your right hand behind you for support. Bring both feet off the ground, draw your legs in toward your chest and hold briefly. Contract the oblique muscles that are facing upward and return to the starting position. Repeat for ten repetitions then switch to the right side. Do not extend your legs all the way out because that stresses the hip flexors and the quads and you want to isolate the muscles you are working. Repeat for ten repetitions.

STOMACH HOLD
Abdominals

Lie face down, in the push-up position, resting on your elbows and toes—making sure not to allow your belly to hang down. Hold abdominals in for five to ten seconds This exercise is not advised for people with back problems. Do ten repetitions.

Exercise No. 19

LAT PULL-DOWNS
Back/Latissimus Dorsi

Extend arms overhead. Pull arms down while squeezing back muscles as hard as you can. Complete ten repetitions.

Exercise No. 20

TWO ARM CURL
Biceps

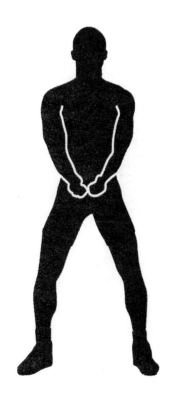 

Standing or sitting upright, palms should be facing up and touching, held slightly below your waist. Curl both arms upward toward your chest and then back down. Repeat for ten repetitions. Make sure not to arch your back, and to squeeze your biceps tightly at the top.

SINGLE ARM CURL
Biceps

Standing or sitting upright, with closed-fist facing up and held slightly below your waist, slowly curl your left arm up toward your chest, flexing your bicep the whole time, then lower your arm. Repeat for ten repetitions, alternating arms.

Exercise No. 22

CHEST SQUEEZE
Chest/Pectorals

Standing or sitting upright, place both hands out in front of your body as if holding a tree and then wrap your arms tightly around your body as you contract your chest muscles. Then open arms wide. Repeat the movement for ten repetitions.

Exercise No. 23

ONE ARM OVER CHEST CROSSOVER
Chest Pectorals

Standing upright with knees bent, push your left arm across your body, while flexing your left pectoral for better focus on the muscle you are working. Place right hand on the left pectoral and push against your chest for better isolation of the muscle. Repeat for ten repetitions then switch to opposite arm for ten repetitions.

ONE ARM ROW
Back/Latissimus Dorsi

Standing with feet about shoulder width apart, place right foot in front of left foot (about 1-1/2 feet), bend at the waist and place your right hand on your right knee, with your left hand at your side. Draw your left arm up, making sure to keep your elbow close to your side. Contract your back muscles and lower hand down. Repeat for ten repetitions, then switch to left leg and hand repeating exercise for ten repetitions.

Exercise No. 25

SIDE LATERAL RAISE
Deltoids/Trapezius

Standing, bend knees and lift both hands up and out to the side, until parallel to the floor, keeping elbows bent. Hold briefly, then lower arms to the side. Repeat for ten repetitions.

Exercise No. 26

SHOULDER PRESS
Trapezius, Deltoids, Triceps and Rhomboids

Standing or sitting upright with hands shoulder height, closed-fist facing forward, push both hands upward without locking out the elbows; then lower hands. Repeat for ten repetitions. Food cans or dumbbells are optional.

Exercise No. 27

UPRIGHT ROW
Trapezius/Rhomboid

Stand with knees bent and holding a brief case if you desire. Exhale as you pull the case up to your chin, bend the elbows, keeping the case close to your body. Pause briefly then lower the case back down concentrating on the stretch of the trapezius muscles. Repeat for ten repetitions. If no case is available, mimic all movements, but concentrate a little harder on feeling the muscles you are working.

SHOULDER ROLLS
Trapezius/Rhomboid

Standing with knees bent, lift shoulders up and roll backwards and down for ten repetitions. Remember to concentrate on contracting your shoulder muscles.

Exercise No. 29

PUSH-UPS
Pectorals, Deltoids and Triceps

Starting in a push-up position with arms about shoulder width apart, back flat and your buttocks down, lower your chest close to the ground and back up for ten repetitions. Remember to exhale as you're pushing upward and to concentrate on the stretch in the chest as you lower your body to the floor.

Exercise No. 30

TRICEP KICKBACK
Triceps

Standing with knees bent and bending over at the waist, body parallel to the floor, keeping knees, elbows close to the body, straighten arms and flex your triceps muscles. Then bend arms back up to starting position. Do this for ten repetitions.

people care more about their homes, and their cars, than they do about keeping their bodies in good shape. I personally hope some day we all will get a revelation in the area of good health. Should this happen, we would spend less time and money on the "stuff" and a lot more to keep our precious bodies in top conditions.

We are all a work in progress—each at a different level of physical fitness. I know several women who would rather spend a few more minutes keeping the house looking like new than keeping up with their fitness workouts. If you want your body to look like no one lives in it, put everything else first! Don't keep your fitness account up to date. Even in the Bible it talks about our bodies as the temple of the Holy Ghost. God says that we are not our own; that we are bought with a price and therefore we should glorify God in body and spirit. We must realize what we do today will not only affect us now, but will also determine what our health will be tomorrow.

Ladies, remember when folding your clothes and ironing out all those wrinkles, there is really only one safe way to diminish those wrinkles around your stomach and waist, and that is through personal exercise. Many times I've talked with people who have told me they cannot stand to look at themselves in a mirror. I tell them they should do something about it and they say they agree and walk away and forget about it. Our bodies are like those bills that come in the mail. If we just look at them, they generally will keep on growing larger with interest, and our bodies are no different!

How do I personally eat?

If you remember reading earlier I said I would talk more with you about diet and nutritional values. For the most part I select a high nutrient food count along with leaner cuts of meat, plenty of fruits, vegetables and whole grains.

Though I do eat well, I would not want to give anyone the impression that I am a perfect eater. Occasionally, I do like to treat myself. Over the years, I've had many people ask me where are some of my favorite places for eating? With all sincerity, I would like to say when I want a great Chicken Ceasar Wrap, I go to the French Meadows bakery in Minneapolis. In the past three years, I've have eaten more great chicken from the French Meadows in Minneapolis than the previous fifteen years. The meat is always tender and wrapped in a healthy tortilla. When I feel like having French fries– which is three to four times a year–I go to Runyon's on Washington Avenue in Minneapolis. I think they have the best fries in town when you get them hot.

When I want a great breakfast I go to the Original Pancake House in Edina, Minnesota. My favorite are the pancakes they call the Forty-niner's. I also love their baked hash browns. If it was not for Caribou and Starbucks, I would not have had any early morning place to go and write this book. I like having a mocha. Remember, I said I believe I can eat what I want some of the time, not all of the time. It's true for me as my livelihood comes from working out and I daily expend more calories than I take in. Calories can be very high in a mocha with whole milk. Staying in shape does have its rewards.

As far as my regular eating is concerned, my favorite foods include, baked salmon, baked chicken, shrimp, grilled asparagus, green beans, broccoli, sweet potatoes, garlic, spinach, tomatoes, and any kind of fruit.

Is your family's health stock increasing?

By now I hope you are concerned for your family's health picture and that you are doing something about it. Let me give you an inside look at my family's good health efforts. Let's start with my family's healthy work out habits. My family's health stock has been great. I was born into a family of seven.

My father, Russell – 79 years young lifts weights three days a week, rides the exercise bike three days a week, can still do two sets of ten repetitions on pull-ups. He has maintained his body weight from the time he was thirty-six, give or take a year or so. Chronologically speaking, my Dad is aging. His health stock is steadily increasing and maintaining this year.

My mother, Rachel – 71 years, rides her bike everyday and physically speaking is in great health. She will often bike from Fridley, which is a northern suburb of Minneapolis, to the south side of Minneapolis just to pick up some healthy food. She has maintained her weight for forty years and I would say that her health stock has not decreased over the years. She is maintaining good health at 71 years old.

My sister, Audreia – age 54, works out three to four times per week and hasn't changed her figure over thirty years. When people see her they are always amazed at her awareness of the fact that she knows its time to invest in her health for the future. Audreia knows that if she wants to continue moving later in life she'll do it now first and keep on going! I would have to say her health stock is increasing, also.

My brother, Russell Jr. – age 53 has always been involved in some physical sport; in high-school, gymnastics, track, Karate, fighting in tournaments and later, opening a Karate school in San Bernardino, California. For a period, my brother was in the real estate business and making a lot of money, forgetting the important things we were taught by our parents–until he had a heart attack. After that, my brother stopped smoking and started to slow down and appreciate his life. Now, at this time, his health stock is slowly on the rise.

Myself – age 52, I ride the exercise bike every other day for approximately forty to sixty minutes, and I weight train every other day. I have, personally, never felt better. I can do things that I could not do when I was twenty-nine years old. My stock is rising as you read this book.

My sister, Rhonda, who grew up running track has always been involved in some type of sporting event. She is active with either volleyball, softball or touch football.

My youngest sister, for personal reasons, does not want her name in print. She is an ice skater, and maintains her health by practicing her sport on a consistent basis. Although she is slightly heavier than she should be, her health stock is doing well.

Where are you and your family? Is your health stock growing, or is it near depletion? Think about where you are in your health issues. While there is still time, take action that will make a difference in the quality of your life.

My oldest sister Audreia Henderson works at being fit.

Hi, my name is Audreia Henderson. I am the oldest of seven children. Fitness has always been a part of my life. My mother was really into track and field activities and I guess it rubbed off onto all of us children. I was never into the competitive end of things as my mother wanted me to be, but I always like the way I would feel when I did any kind of physical activities. It carried on for my own family also when I had my children.

I also believed early in my life it was important to take care of myself. Now even though I'm older, I feel as if I'm in the best shape I've ever been. People ask me how I do what I do very often. I'm in such good shape, I usually say some of it is good genes, but for the most part, I didn't abuse my body like most people do. People I saw while growing up, were smoking and drinking too much at a very young age. Later on in years, it wore on their bodies with heavy damage to their lives.

I exercise regularly, try to keep eating right, and have a positive attitude. I believe it is important to start while you are young, doing some kind of physical activity, whether it is walking, running, riding a bike, swimming– anything that will get the heart pumping and the blood flowing. The best thing now is you can start no matter what your age. It is never too late to **exercise, breathe and live**. *If you can still move, do it."*

May the end of this book become a new chapter in your life. I trust you will become, and stay, physically fit for the balance of your days here on earth. May you be physically and spiritually alive for the rest of your days.
Ron Henderson

P.S. Be assured, I will be delighted to hear from you about your quest toward a healthy lifestyle. Please write me your thoughts regarding your journey. Ron@fitnessking.com

Track and Feel Record

Physical activities completed And time spent in activity	Time Hr/Min	How did you feel after the activity?
Mon		
Tues		
Wed		
Thu		
Fri		
Sat		
Sun		

Track and Feel Record

Physical activities completed And time spent in activity	Time Hr/Min	How did you feel after the activity?
Mon		
Tues		
Wed		
Thu		
Fri		
Sat		
Sun		

Track and Feel Record

Physical activities completed And time spent in activity		Time Hr/Min		How did you feel after the activity?			
Mon							
Tues							
Wed							
Thu							
Fri							
Sat							
Sun							

Track and Feel Record

Physical activities completed And time spent in activity		Time Hr/Min		How did you feel after the activity?			
Mon							
Tues							
Wed							
Thu							
Fri							
Sat							
Sun							

Track and Feel Record

Physical activities completed And time spent in activity		Time		How did you feel after the activity?
		Hr/Min		
Mon				
Tues				
Wed				
Thu				
Fri				
Sat				
Sun				

Track and Feel Record

Physical activities completed And time spent in activity		Time		How did you feel after the activity?
		Hr/Min		
Mon				
Tues				
Wed				
Thu				
Fri				
Sat				
Sun				

Track and Feel Record

Physical activities completed And time spent in activity | **How did you feel after the activity?**

	Time			
		Hr/Min		
Mon				
Tues				
Wed				
Thu				
Fri				
Sat				
Sun				

Track and Feel Record

Physical activities completed And time spent in activity | **How did you feel after the activity?**

	Time			
		Hr/Min		
Mon				
Tues				
Wed				
Thu				
Fri				
Sat				
Sun				

Track and Feel Record

Physical activities completed And time spent in activity	Time		How did you feel after the activity?
	Hr/Min		
Mon			
Tues			
Wed			
Thu			
Fri			
Sat			
Sun			

Track and Feel Record

Physical activities completed And time spent in activity	Time		How did you feel after the activity?
	Hr/Min		
Mon			
Tues			
Wed			
Thu			
Fri			
Sat			
Sun			

-97-

Track and Feel Record

Physical activities completed And time spent in activity	Time		How did you feel after the activity?	
		Hr/Min		
Mon				
Tues				
Wed				
Thu				
Fri				
Sat				
Sun				

Track and Feel Record

Physical activities completed And time spent in activity	Time		How did you feel after the activity?	
		Hr/Min		
Mon				
Tues				
Wed				
Thu				
Fri				
Sat				
Sun				

Track and Feel Record

Physical activities completed And time spent in activity	Time		How did you feel after the activity?
	Hr/Min		
Mon			
Tues			
Wed			
Thu			
Fri			
Sat			
Sun			

Track and Feel Record

Physical activities completed And time spent in activity	Time		How did you feel after the activity?
	Hr/Min		
Mon			
Tues			
Wed			
Thu			
Fri			
Sat			
Sun			

Track and Feel Record

Physical activities completed And time spent in activity

How did you feel after the activity?

Time

		Hr/Min	
Mon			
Tues			
Wed			
Thu			
Fri			
Sat			
Sun			

Track and Feel Record

Physical activities completed And time spent in activity

How did you feel after the activity?

Time

		Hr/Min	
Mon			
Tues			
Wed			
Thu			
Fri			
Sat			
Sun			

Track and Feel Record

Physical activities completed And time spent in activity | **Time** | **How did you feel after the activity?**

Physical activities completed And time spent in activity	Hr/Min		How did you feel after the activity?
Mon			
Tues			
Wed			
Thu			
Fri			
Sat			
Sun			

Track and Feel Record

Physical activities completed And time spent in activity | **Time** | **How did you feel after the activity?**

Physical activities completed And time spent in activity	Hr/Min		How did you feel after the activity?
Mon			
Tues			
Wed			
Thu			
Fri			
Sat			
Sun			

Track and Feel Record

Physical activities completed And time spent in activity | **How did you feel after the activity?**

	Time		How did you feel after the activity?
	Hr/Min		
Mon			
Tues			
Wed			
Thu			
Fri			
Sat			
Sun			

Track and Feel Record

Physical activities completed And time spent in activity | **How did you feel after the activity?**

	Time		How did you feel after the activity?
	Hr/Min		
Mon			
Tues			
Wed			
Thu			
Fri			
Sat			
Sun			

Track and Feel Record

Physical activities completed And time spent in activity

Time

How did you feel after the activity?

		Hr/Min			
Mon					
Tues					
Wed					
Thu					
Fri					
Sat					
Sun					

Track and Feel Record

Physical activities completed And time spent in activity

Time

How did you feel after the activity?

		Hr/Min			
Mon					
Tues					
Wed					
Thu					
Fri					
Sat					
Sun					

Track and Feel Record

Physical activities completed And time spent in activity

	Time Hr/Min		How did you feel after the activity?				
Mon							
Tues							
Wed							
Thu							
Fri							
Sat							
Sun							

Track and Feel Record

Physical activities completed And time spent in activity

	Time Hr/Min		How did you feel after the activity?				
Mon							
Tues							
Wed							
Thu							
Fri							
Sat							
Sun							

Track and Feel Record

Physical activities completed And time spent in activity	Time Hr/Min		How did you feel after the activity?
Mon			
Tues			
Wed			
Thu			
Fri			
Sat			
Sun			

Track and Feel Record

Physical activities completed And time spent in activity	Time Hr/Min		How did you feel after the activity?
Mon			
Tues			
Wed			
Thu			
Fri			
Sat			
Sun			

Track and Feel Record

Physical activities completed And time spent in activity	Time	How did you feel after the activity?
	Hr/Min	
Mon		
Tues		
Wed		
Thu		
Fri		
Sat		
Sun		

Track and Feel Record

Physical activities completed And time spent in activity	Time	How did you feel after the activity?
	Hr/Min	
Mon		
Tues		
Wed		
Thu		
Fri		
Sat		
Sun		

Track and Feel Record

Physical activities completed And time spent in activity

Time

How did you feel after the activity?

	Hr/Min		
Mon			
Tues			
Wed			
Thu			
Fri			
Sat			
Sun			

Track and Feel Record

Physical activities completed And time spent in activity

Time

How did you feel after the activity?

	Hr/Min		
Mon			
Tues			
Wed			
Thu			
Fri			
Sat			
Sun			

Track and Feel Record

Table 1

Physical activities completed And time spent in activity	Time Hr/Min	How did you feel after the activity?
Mon		
Tues		
Wed		
Thu		
Fri		
Sat		
Sun		

Track and Feel Record

Table 2

Physical activities completed And time spent in activity	Time Hr/Min	How did you feel after the activity?
Mon		
Tues		
Wed		
Thu		
Fri		
Sat		
Sun		